When the Banshee Howls
and other poems

Other books by John W. Leys:
The Darkness of His Dreams: Poetry (2019)
Whispers of a One-Eyed Raven: Mythological Poetry (2020)

Other books containing poetry by John W. Leys:
All the Lonely People by Nicholas Gagnier (2019)

Avalanches in Poetry: Poetry, Stories, and Art Inspired by Leonard Cohen, edited by David L. O'Nan (2019)

As the World Burns: Writers and Artists Reflect on a World Gone Mad, edited by Kindra M. Austin, Candice Louisa Daquin, Rachel Finch, and Christine E. Ray (Indie Blu(e), 2020)

Through the Looking Glass – Reflecting on the Madness and Chaos Within, edited by Kindra M. Austin, Candice Louisa Daquin, John W. Leys, Christine E. Ray, and Marcia Weber (Indie Blu(e), 2021)

When the Banshee Howls
And other poems

John W. Leys

Broken Wing Publishing
Albany, Oregon

2022 - 5783

Copyright © 2022 John W. Leys

All rights reserved. No part of this publication may be reproduced, distributed, or transmitted in any form by any means, including photocopying, recording, or other electronic methods without the prior written permission of the author, except in the case of brief quotations embodied in reviews and certain other noncommercial uses permitted by copyright law.

Many the poems in this collection first appeared, in earlier revisions, on http://johnwleys.com/

'Silence Falls,' Solitary Confinement,' 'Darkness and Fog,' and 'Defenses Down' were originally published in *Through the Looking Glass – Reflecting on the Madness and Chaos Within* (Indie Blu(e), 2021)

'It's Getting Darker' was originally published in *Avalanches of Poetry Inspired by Leonard Cohen* edited by David L. O'Nan (2019)

Cover Design by John W. Leys
Cover Photo by Plato Terentev
Illustrations by John W. Leys
All Photos taken by John W. Leys, except for the photos on pgs. 34-37 are from the Leys Family Archive
The Unified Heart on pg. 75 was designed by Leonard Cohen.
The Infinite Heart was designed by John W Leys
The drawing in the photo on pg. 91 is by Leah Doan

ISBN: 978-1-7333645-4-6 (Paperback)

Library of Congress Control Number: 2022918408

First Published:22 November 2022 by Broken Wing Publishing

In memory of
Rabbi Joel Wasser Z"L
1963-2014

I miss you, my holy friend
- JWL

לזכרה של
הרב יקב זלמן בן יחודה ורכל ז"ל
5724-5774

אני מתגעגע אליך ידידי הקדוש
- אליהו בן אברהם ושרה

I don't need people
To Remember me
When I'm gone

I just want
Someone
To notice

JWL 2018

Contents

WHEN THE BANSHEE HOWLS 11

The Journey Home 13
- An Exodus Long Overdue 15
- The Wild 17
- Homeward Bound 19
- The Love Song of a Lost Raven 20
- אליהו הנביא 22

Sailing into the West 25
- The Empty House – a Tanka 27
- Haunted 28
- I Can Still Feel You 31
- Silence Falls 32
- When the Banshee Howls 34
- Down the Tracks 38
- מזמור לאליהו המשורר 39
- On This Day I Completed My 46th Year 41

Poets & Madmen 45
- Poets 47
- Vincent 48
- The Mad Poet 50

Broken Hearts 53
- Running Away 55
- Waiting for the Rain 57
- We Began Breaking Up Before We Ever Met 58
- The Old Dirt Road 60
- Our First Kiss 61
- Broken Hearts 63

It's Getting Darker 65
- Burning Flame—a troilet 67
- No Time Given 68
- A Flash of the Lightening 69
- Bloody Battlefield 70
- Lancelot's Wound 71
- Old Ragged Suit 72
- Solitary Confinement 73
- It's Getting Darker 74
- Darkness and Fog 76

Defenses Down	78
I Can't Reach You	80
A Twitch Away From the End	81
Free Falling	82
Out of the Shadows	*87*
Out of the Shadows	89
Accidental Daughter	90
My Heart's in the Highlands	92
I Am Yours	*95*
To Whom It May Concern	97
Ripples	98
Freckles and Curls	100
A Different Kind of Treaty	104
Live and Love	107
Always	108
Tangled Up in You	110
My Irish Princess	111
All Things Must Pass	*113*
The Little Black Notebook	115

ACKNOWLEDGMENTS ... 117

ABOUT THE AUTHOR ... 123

When the Banshee Howls

The Journey Home

An Exodus Long Overdue

I pulled out of the gas station
Under a grey March sky,
A hot chai in the cupholder.

Turning down the old highway
Past the frozen trees that bear no leaves,
Beyond the Sisters standing sentry,
Into the valley below.

Dylan's divorce soundtracks
My journey home
To the land of my father;
The home of my mother:
A haunted mausoleum
Decorated in wood paneling.

If you live there long enough
The wilderness can feel like home,
And home a foreign country,
Desolate as the Sinai desert;
Dark as the shadows cast
By the trees in Celyddon's wood.

11/11/21

Into the wilderness
Into the wild
Without a single luxury
Open to anything
Seeing everything
is unknown

only then
only there
Can one hear
the still soft voice speaking
from the bush that burns
but is not consumed

The Wild

Into the Wilderness,
Into the wild
Without a single luxury.
Open to anything
Because everything is unknown.

Only there can one hear
The still soft voice
From the bush that burns,
But is not consumed.

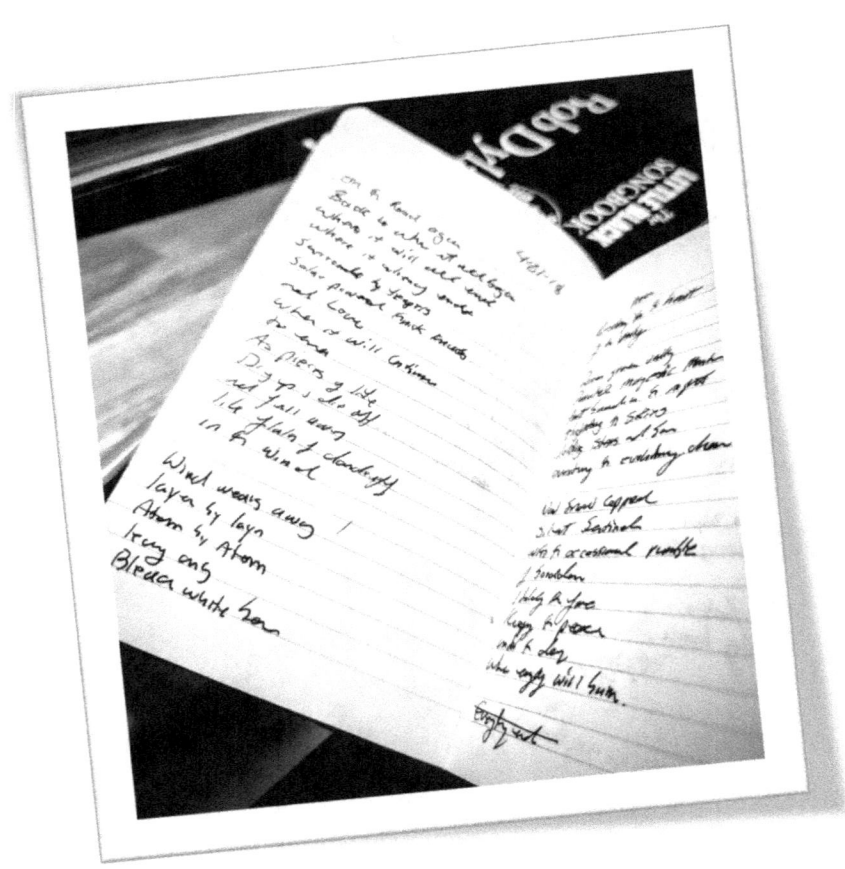

Homeward Bound

On the road again
Back to where it all began,
Where it will all end,
Where it already ended;
Where it is still ending
As pieces of life
Dry up, die off,
And fall away
Like flakes of dandruff
In the wind.

The wind wears away
Layer by layer
Atom by atom
Leaving only
Bleached white bones
Resting near the heart
Of the valley.

River green valley
Parallel the majestic mountains
That burned in the night,
Lighting the skies,
Blotting stars and Sun,
Overturning the evolutionary chain.

Now snowcapped silent sentinels,
With the occasional rumble of boredom,
Holding fire, keeping the peace
Until the day
When everything will burn.

The Love Song of a Lost Raven
For TS Eliot

And then I went
All on my own
Knowing for sure now
That nothing is carved in stone.

Nothing lasts,
Everything ends.
Sanity largely hinges
On the color of one's lens.

Nothing seems as it should
Nothing happened as expected.
Though the choices were foreshadowed early,
And demand to be respected.

April is cruel,
But July's no picnic either:
Endings, beginnings, and birthdays,
The wheat's waiting for the reaper.

The heavens draw darker
As the sun into the west descends.
The future grows shorter
As my hair greys and thins.

Follow Helios' chariot
To the valley where ravens have flown,
Dim and dusky dirt roads
I must forever walk alone.

אליהו הנביא
Eliyahu HaNavi[1]

Frightened, I flee
For my life,
Dismissing my manservant,
Escaping into the wilderness
Where our fathers wandered
In the presence of God.

Settling under a juniper bush
I pray the Lord take my life.

Am I a righteous Enoch
That I should ascend to Heaven
While I still breathe
And not join my fathers
As dust returns to dust?

I am Noah,
Blameless in my generation,
Though my generation
Is a vile pit of sin.
There will be no flood
To drown the wicked,
And no Ark to rescue me.

In the night
My prayers are answered,
But it's not the answer I wished for.
A messenger gives me
A hot meal
And directions.

---

[1] Elijah the Prophet

I journey into the past
In the time it takes
To drown a world,
I arrive at the plane
Where the golden idol
Was raised,
And holy blood was spilt.
I climb the mountain
Where the Law took form,
Sit in a cave and wait,
Alone,
Isolated by my faith.

In the morning,
Beckoned by my Liege,
I come into the daylight,
Feel the wind in my hair,
Feel the mountain move
Beneath my feet,
And feel the heat of fire
On my face.
A still small voice
Whispers in my ear.

I must return home.

Sailing into the West

The Empty House – a Tanka

In an empty house
Short stools; covered up mirrors
Filled with a spirit,
A shade that will never leave,
Shadows that will never lift.

Haunted

Walking an old path
Down aging concrete,
Grayer than memory allows,
Each crack as familiar
As the crease of my palm,
Volcanoes and lightning strikes,
Slowly stepping back in time.

Great pine tree,
Full of crow caws
And raven whispers
That I answered
On my way to school.

Now as silent
As a schoolyard
In summertime.

They're selling sub sandwiches
Where the arcade used to be,
And baking pizzas
In the old Datsun showroom,
The lot too big for the business.

There's a hole in the house,
Where you used to be,
On the left side of the couch
Next to your teacup,
Smarties, and Kindle.

There's always a chill
When I sit in that spot,
Sipping chai tea
From your cup,
Remembering
When you were here.

*Walking back
into memories
of sidewalk concrete
Seen a little older
a little more grey
A crack a little deeper
A sign a bit taller
Comfortingly different
Strangely familiar.

Everything has changed
except of you
but are exactly
the same.*

8-29-18

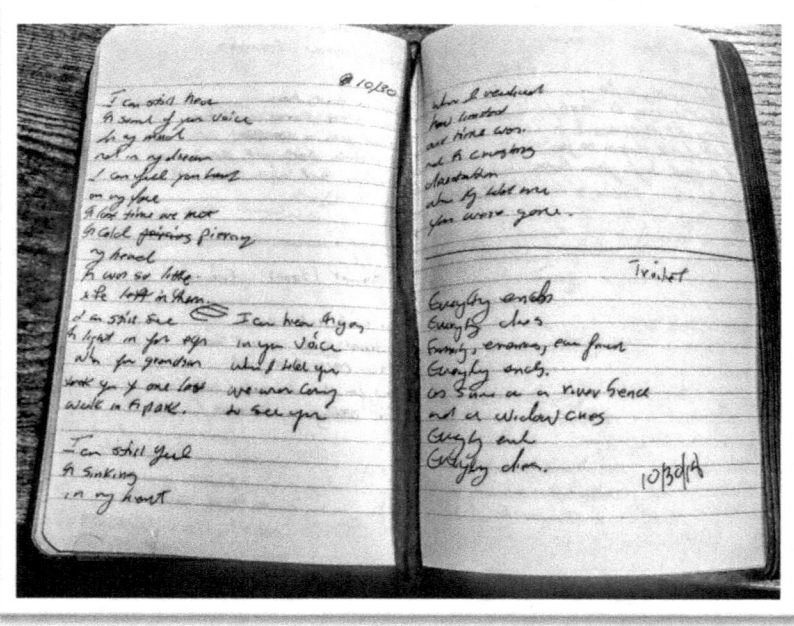

I Can Still Feel You

I can still hear
The sound of your voice
In my mind
And in my dreams.
I can feel your hands on my face
The last time we met,
The cold piercing my beard,
There was so little life left in them.

I can hear the joy
In your voice
When I told you
We were coming to see you.
I can still see the light in your eyes
When your grandson took you for one last
Walk in the park.

I can still feel
The sinking in my heart
When I realized
How limited our time really was,
And the crushing devastation
When they told me
You were gone.

Silence Falls

I lost my voice in the fog,
Crushed by the darkness
On which it once fed.

I lost her
And my soul poured out,
Page after page,
Until every tear rhymed.

I lost him
And the well slowly dried up,
As I tumbled down
Like Alice,
Forever falling,
Never landing,
Tears streaming,
Silently screaming,
Until broken
At the bottom
I came to land.

I tried to cry,
But I couldn't breathe.
I tried to die,
But I couldn't leave
My boy, my light,
The only life I still had
To live for.

The air was
Oppressive and thick,
Like Tampa in August.
Barely breathing,
I couldn't speak,

I held my broken cup
And prayed for rain,
Soothing cool relief,
To let me sing again.

When the Banshee Howls
For Patricia Spoon (1940-2021)

I heard the banshee
Wailing in the distance,
Echoing in the valley,
Weeping among the
Rose covered hills of Montrose.
The bagpipes whisper a dirge,
Drifting from Angus
To the Highlands,
Welcoming another soul
Coming home.

Aunt Pat

I remember
A feisty single mother
Of five children
Of various shapes,
Sizes, and temperaments.

I remember broken windows,
Duct tape, and color coded
Christmas presents.

I remember a cherry red
Volkswagen bug
That was hit by a deer.
And I remember you
Insisting the sheriff call a vet
Instead of putting the animal down.

I remember love.

I remember the wit
And the snark;
Holding your own
Against the two clowns
You had for brothers,
Hanging up the phone
When you'd had enough.

I remember love.

I remember the losses:
Your mother,
Your husband, your son,
Grandson, and your brothers too.

I remember love.

Dad, Pat, and Wally

Dad, Aunt Pat & Uncle Wally

*Aunt Pat,
Grandma Leys,
& Dad.*

I remember never giving up,
Never giving in,
Fighting while there
Was still fight left.
Even when you started
Losing yourself.

I remember love.

Aunt Pat, Grandma Leys, Uncle Wally, and Dad.

I heard the banshee wailing
And felt her tears
Blowing in the wind,
Her voice as familiar
As the pain I now feel,
Her presence like that
Of an old friend.

I heard the banshee wailing,
I heard the bagpipes dirging,
With roses over their heads
And God's good earth
Beneath their backs,
Welcoming another soul home.

Down the Tracks

Life is not a road
On which we walk.
Roads can be walked
In either direction.

Life is a train
On which we ride,
Traveling forward
At faster
And faster speeds
Until we reach
Our destination.

מזמור לאליהו המשורר
A Psalm of Eliyahu HaMeshorer[2]

What is man
That you should take notice of him,
A son of man
That you should be concerned with him,
Elevating him far above
The other beasts of the field

Man is dust,
Less than a breath,
A son of man
Is an illusion,
A passing shadow
In the flickering heat
Of the sun.

---

[2] Elijah the Poet

January 22d 1824.

Missolonghi

On this day I complete my thirty
sixth year. —

1.
'Tis time this heart should be unmoved
 Since others it hath ceased to move.
Yet though I cannot be beloved
 Still let me love!

2.
My days are in the yellow leaf
 The flowers and fruits of love are gone
The worm — the canker, and the grief
 Are mine alone! —

3.
The fire that on my bosom preys
 Is lone as some Volcanic Isle
No torch is kindled at its blaze
 A funeral pile!

4.
The hope, the fear, the jealous care,
 The exalted portion of the pain
And power of Love I cannot share

On This Day I Completed My 46th Year

I woke up this morning
With fewer steps ahead
Then there are behind,
As the incline increases
In proportion to the number
Of familiar faced corpses
Rotting in the ditch
Along the side of the road.

Bone on bone
Cartilage-free grinding
In my knees
Won't hold out much longer.
Though they've lasted
Ten years longer
Then Byron's club foot,
Marching a Grecian swamp
In search of a soldier's grave
To lie down in.

Forty-Six years
And both my parents are gone,
My own sunset in sight,
Nihilism scratching
The inside of my skull.
Drifting in the dusk,
Memories of motivations
And dreams unseen
Flutter and fade,
Smoke in the sky.

Shadows on the Sea

The shadow stretches
And grows as the sun sets
Into the sea, until all is darkness.

From daybreak until dusk
The clock ticks
Tocks, clicks
Down to the docks.

Seconds and minutes
March in formation,
Precise, steady,
A perfect procession,
Never deterred from the destination.

Inevitable, equitable,
Never early or late,
Arriving just when it means to:

At Camlann,
In London Tower;
On the Senate floor.

In an Athenian jail,
A Dakota doorway;
An Iowa cornfield.

At Missolonghi,
In a Paris apartment;
On board the *Ariel*[3]
Sailing into the west.

---

[3] Or was it the *Don Juan*?

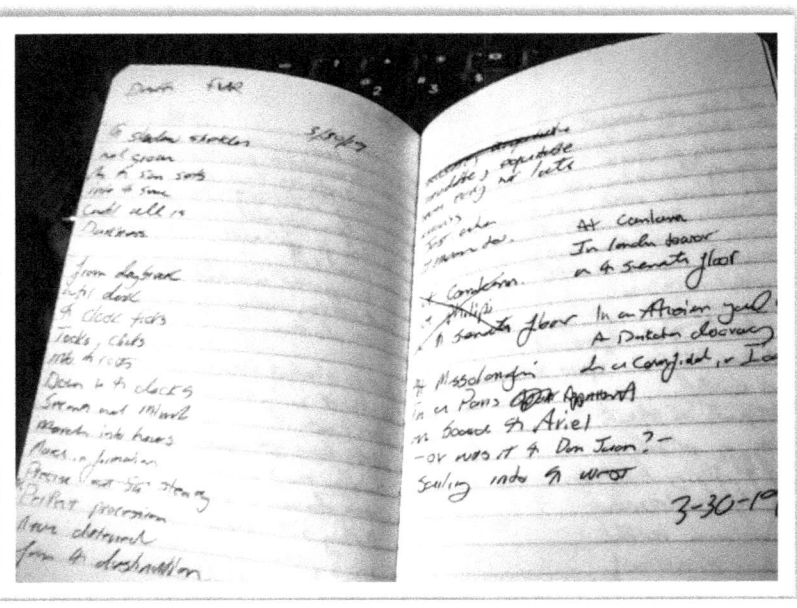

Poets & Madmen

Poets

Poets are packrats
and magpies,
scavengers and gravediggers.
They are ghosts
that haunt themselves
with melancholy and murder
—metaphorically—
martyring themselves
for selfish selfless reasons.

Poets are liars
and madmen,
lunatics and
Shakespearean fools.
They are Ezekiel,
describing wheels within wheels
with Cassandra's voice.
they are noble born vagabonds
and working-class kings.

Poets are blind bards
describing the divine
as seen with their soul.
They whisper thunder
and shout silence,
listening only
to that still soft voice
that rides on the wind.

Vincent

Driving rain down to Arles
to the ginger artist
with the wild eyes,
painting the air currents
and perceiving everyday ecstasy,
canvas and brushes in hand,
in the face of failure
and the weight of darkness,
shimmering scenes and
pigment poems
washing over the landscape,
ordinary beauty & hidden hope,
shining in the swirling stars
seen beyond the asylum windows.

The Mad Poet

Mad Pollyanna poet
Depressed
In love with the night,
Admirer of the stars,
Constellations, and galaxies,
The milky white way
Against the raven black
Echoes of eternity,
Heart hardwired
To the planet's pulse.
Feel the continents drift
Under your feet,
Between the clicks of the clock.

Self-martyring madman,
Preparing a sacrifice
At Aphrodite's altar,
Attended by the nine daughters of Zeus,
Razor ready to bleed India ink
On the sacred scrolls and tablets.

Damaged, hurt; heartbroken,
Looking on the bright side
Of the silver lining,
Believing—despite the darkness
That light still exists.

Mad Hattering,
March Hare tea partying,
Cheshire smile that lingers
Long after he's faded away.

Broken Hearts

Running Away

You can run
Across dead leaves,
Through naked trees
In a dusk lit woodland
Off the trail,
Away from the crowd,
But you'll never
Outrun your past
Without tripping
Over your destiny.

1-11-22

I remember the first time I sold pot
Kneeling beneath Tree
In the center of the garden
I'm offered a choice
explained the consequences
and I rose like a coward.

Waiting for the Rain

Kneeling in the wet grass
Among the rotten crab apples,
Beneath the tree in the center of the garden.

An offer, a choice.
Consequences and cowardice.

Walking into the Wilderness,
The great tree burning like a flaming sword,
Scorched earth and blackened grass
Broken dreams and oaken ash,
And an empty cracked clay cup
Waiting for the rain.

We Began Breaking Up Before We Ever Met

Smokey dim lit pool hall--
Red lights making volcanic plumes
Of loneliness, desperation, and shame--
Next to a brittle brown pine tree
A quarter mile off the grey gravel road
In the shadow of Interstate Five

Rusted vomit-soaked jukebox
Softly singing *Sgt Pepper* and *Imagine*
To half empty dance floor of wallflowers,
Lost souls and broken hearts.
World weary alcohol-soaked Army veterans and
Naive intellectual freshman English majors
Cling to one another, boa constrictor grip: Afraid
Of solitude, depression and dying alone in an empty
apartment.
Distorted delusional visions of idealized lovers:
Never changing, never disappointing, never existing.

Experimentation, shampoo lube and 3,000 miles later,
Living twin bed fucking in off-campus squalor.
Catholic Hare Krishna Taoist correcting
School newspaper editorial grammar.
Noahite Indiana Jones finding lost Ark,
Signing covenants with blood dripping from a
bleeding penis.
A relationship as smooth as an infected diaper rash.

Bright clear sunlit college courtyard
Spring flowers bloom, feral cats in heat,
Gulf winds blow carefully chosen rational reasons
Putting a bullet in the head of a rabid dog.

Before the breeze could clear brimstone smog
Soldier boots hit pavement,
Tactical retreat, regroup, prepare for next engagement.
She sits there alone,
Slightly disappointed
that he left
Just like she told him to.

We started breaking up
Before we'd even met
In that little roadside music ha[ll]
Down the dirt road off Interstate

The man you fell in love with
Was never really me
And he was never anybody
I ever really wanted to be

I don't hate myself
For loving you,
But I've come close

It all came crashing down
In the courtyards of academia,
Too public a place to cause a sc[ene]
Calculated rationa[l]

The Old Dirt Road

I left you sitting
by the side of that old dirt road
Near the place we lived together
For so many years

But you never got up
To dust yourself off,
Wander off,
And see if the rest of
The road was paved.

You built a cabin
Out of deadwood
Laying on the side of the road
Flagging down
Every lonesome traveler who passed by,
Marrying the first one who stayed.

I'm 40 miles gone now
Living down past
Where the dirt road hits the highway
Never staying anywhere for long
But no longer staying anywhere alone.

Our First Kiss

You kissed me with just your lips,
A pleasant yet passionless red flag,
Invisible to colourblind eyes.

You never kissed me the way that *she* did:

Tongues darting,
Desperately devouring,
Tasting teeth and gums,
Intensity increasing
'til conscious thought gives way
To Passion-soaked instinct and ecstasy.

You never kissed me like *that*.

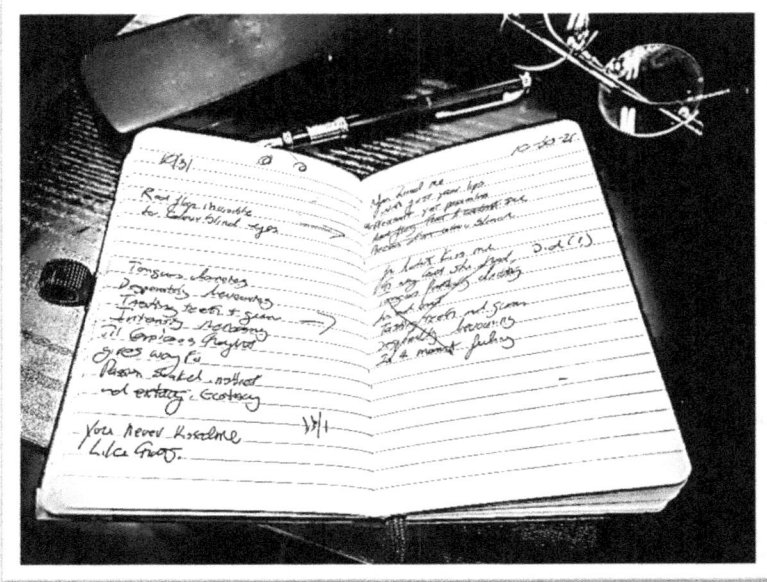

Broken Hearts
For TS Eliot

We are the broken men
We hold our broken hearts,
We are the stupid men
Chasing those stupid tarts.

See the hollow man
With his hollow soul
Gazing at the dawn
Wishing to be whole.

See the golden angel
With her golden hair
Wondering what broke him
If there's any hope of repair

See the golden light
Reflected from golden wings
The source of salvation
Of which the singer sings

See those stupid men,
Moaning dirge-like tunes
Crying, rubbing salt
In their self-inflicted wounds.

These are the broken men
Clutching their broken hearts,
Trapped in the plays they wrote
Dutifully playing their broken parts.

It's Getting Darker

Burning Flame—a troilet

Candle flame brightly burned,
Extinguished, blackened; cold.
Through the seasons as they turned
Candle flame brightly burned,
Illuminating lessons learned:
Not always doing as you're told.
Candle flame brightly burned,
Extinguished, blackened; cold.

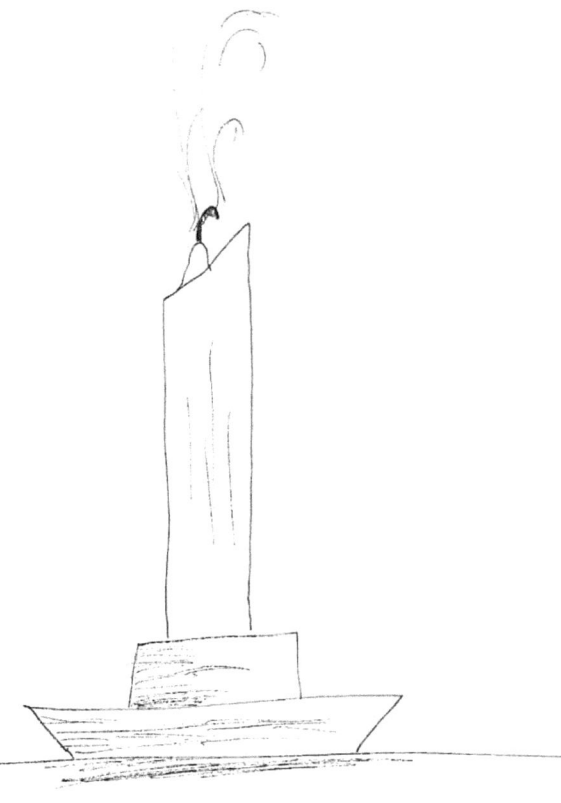

No Time Given

No time given,
Only time taken.

Taken by the alarm clock
Taken by the timeclock,
Taken by paperwork,
Client calls and writing receipts.
Taken for forced smiles
And wondering why
The boss is in a mood today.
Taken by the grocery store,
The gas station, and
Rush hour traffic.

Taken by exhaustion,
And that stabbing pain
In the back of my knee.
Taken by cleaning the house,
Dirty dishes,
And The cat box is full again…

Taken to try and unwind,
Relax and recover from
The emotional and auditory
Overload fuzzing neurons
Like a 22" B&W TV
With broken rabbit ears.

A Flash of the Lightening

The years go flying by
Like shooting stars,
A flash,
A motion in the sky,
And then they're gone.

Yesterday,
 I stood before you
And bared my soul.
Today I sit alone,
Broken and cold.

I never thought
To be here again,
But I should have known
It would happen.
It's a familiar place
No one should visit:
The walls are drafty.
The mirrors broken,
The only reflection I see
Is my own.

I need you here
To hold me,
'cos I'm falling
And I don't know when
I'll stop.

Bloody Battlefield

An old weary soldier,
Alone on an empty battlefield,
Mud filled trenches and
Bombed out craters.
Still smoldering fires in the distance.
Every other soul,
Friend or foe,
Felled along the line.

A brief pause,
After the battle is spent.
In tattered clothes,
He talks to ghosts,
Debating with Death
To lay down arms forever
Before the conflict continues.

Lancelot's Wound

On the field at Camlann,
Lancelot lays bleeding,
Though not a single sword
Scratched his plated armor.

"'Tis the old wound, Sire,
It has never healed."

"Because of your sin,
Sir Lancelot?"

"No, Sire,
Because I kept
Picking at it."

Old Ragged Suit

The threads are loose
And unravelling,
The seams have split,
Barely holding on.

The belt no longer
Holds up the trousers,
Even on the tightest notch.

Failure is inevitable,
The fraying will never stop.
No seamstress
Can repair the damage,
The whole suit is lost.

Solitary Confinement

Disconnected,
Isolated: Alone
In a crowded room.
Avoiding eye contact,
Yet yearning for a touch.
Afraid of the judgment
When they realize
What I really am.

It's Getting Darker
For Leonard Cohen Z"L (1934-2016)

I searched for salvation
I yearned for the light,
Looking for the stars
In the cloud covered night.

I fold my prayer like origami
And stuff it in the crack,
A missive to the almighty
Asking if the Flame is ever coming back.

I close my eyes, reaching out
Caressing the cold aging stone,
Trying to touch the ancient past
My soul has come to call home.

The Temple is in shambles
The Mercy Seat is lost,
2,000 years of homelessness
Trying to tally up the cost.

Looking past Mt. Moriah
To the light of the rising sun,
Warming windblown faces,
Dreams of a suffering undone.

The Messiah isn't coming,
To save this damsel in distress,
It's an uncomfortable truth to which
We cannot fail to acquiesce.

The clouds are growing darker,
But the deluge will never come,
The promise made on rainbow light
Will never be undone.

I yearned for salvation,
Searching for the light,
Is there nothing here to greet me
Save the unending darkness of the night?

Darkness and Fog

The darkness never breaks,
The shadows never lift.
Thoughts flutter in fog
Like lost moths
Unable to escape.

The weight of anxieties,
—real or otherwise—
Press down like a cinder block,
No way for the pressure
To release.

A conspiracy of ravens
And a murder of crows
Flock in the trees
Beyond the yard.
Who are they here for?

Disconnected,
Adrift in the gray.
Bright colors of life
Muted by dense fog,
Murmuring voices
Talking around
And through,
But never to me.

9 Oct 14

a Dozen hours breath
a shadow never lifts
thought flutters in fog
moves to escape

a weight fell
in anxiety
unfurls & real
presses down
like a cinder block
no way to pressen
to relieve,

a luke warm empty
fills every vein
body smells sweet
symmetry
not even to
garden joy pain

Defenses Down

Twilight at the border
Between dark and light,
At the foothills of Dream,
When the walls between
Wake and sleep are thin.

Body and mind relaxed,
Defenses down,
Filters off.

They're waiting for me
In the darkness,
Lingering in the shadows,
Whispering in my ear,
A chorus of lies.

Pulling me down
With the thoughts
I dare not think
In daylight.

Threatening to loose
The Demon
Screaming in my skull,
Lashing out in pain and fear,
The raging beast
I cannot keep caged,
Whose undiluted venom
Will destroy anything
In its path,
Including me.

Sitting on the edge
Of the bed,
Shadows wrapped around
My shoulders,
Weighing me down
Like a cold and wet
Woolen blanket
That was left out
In the rain,
Smelling of mold
And death.

No sleep,
No rest.
Kept awake
By the cacophony,
Whispering within,
Reminding me
Of every ill-spoken word,
Every mistake,
Every awkward interaction,
Every reason
Why nobody will miss me
When I'm gone.

Worn, weary; weeping.
Thinking through molasses
In muted shades of grey.

No fear,
No existential dread,
Yet unable to muster
The energy
To open a vein.

I Can't Reach You

I don't know where you are.
I call out your name in the dark,
And am answered with an echo.

I reach out for you
And grab nothing but the air.
A claustrophobic tightening of the chest
Brings me slowly to my knees.

Behind closed eyes
All I can see is you.
Haunting, hopeful,
And once more out of reach

A Twitch Away From the End

The cold taste of steel,
The faint scent of gunpowder

Just a shiver
On the trigger
And a hot wad of lead
Tears a hole
Severing the cerebellum,
Bringing an end to everything,
Except the darkness.

Free Falling

Throat shredding Banshee scream,
Escaping, echoing down the silent streets at midnight,
Wailing a warning: The Lady in Black stands by.

Pain piercing the hollow chasm
Hiding behind the gap
Between the third and the fourth ribs.

Thoughts swirling
Sinking slowly inward,
Floating free within the walls of the fortress.

Free falling
        down
                down
                        down
                        Choking tears,
                        Hearing blind silent screams
                        Murmuring pain,
                        Chanted like a Hebrew prayer
                        in Brooklyn.
Abyss wrapping,
Cocoon containing
A brilliant despair
Feeding on a dead dream.

Deep sea ear popping pressure,
Slowly soul crushing
For two score and ten,
Arthritic joints ache, aging knees crack and burn.
Fingers tingle, toes grow numb,
Saltwater stings; vision blurs.

I'm tired.
Just tired.
No more spoons; no more strength.
Make. It. Stop.
Please, just make it stop.
Please,
      just
          let
              me
                  go...

Death walked up behind me,
Gentle hand on my shoulder,
Whispering
"I'm sorry, not yet."
And then she was gone.

Out of the Shadows

Out of the Shadows

Under the shadows,
On worn out knees,
Shivering, suffering,
Praying for a way out.
Waiting for Gadot,
Sir Lancelot, or even Don Quixote,
But nothing arrives,
But darkness.

Yet no shadow exists
Without a light
To cast it.
Sunshine over the shoulder,
Nothing but darkness
In sight.
No knight needed
To turn and face the sun.

Accidental Daughter
For Leah

You're exactly what I never knew I needed:
Ascending angel, accidentally adopted;
Adored and treasured.
Not fallen, but torn down and pushed
By lesser demons undeserving of the light.

You held my hand in the fog
Until I could find my way out,
Discovering pieces of me I'd thought
Forever lost in the battle for my soul.

Our paths didn't cross, they merged
The freeway blending into the Interstate:
Inseparable,
Disappearing down the horizon,
Where the path becomes a point,
And the future is born.

My Heart's in the Highlands
*(Inspired by 'My Heart's in the Highlands' by Robert Burns
& 'Highlands' by Bob Dylan)*

My heart's in the Highlands, my heart isn't here,
Chasing white rabbits; following the deer
Down the hill past the magpies at play
My heart's in the Highlands
Straining to hear what they say

Singing from oak branches,
    a half-remembered rhyme,
Drawing upon images from a far better time.
Walking from Stonehaven to Montrose by the sea,
My heart's in the Highlands,
Unburdened and free.

Fatherless children with their grandfather's name,
Bound together like links in a golden chain.
Reaching back in time, over land, over sea,
Reaching back to the Highlands
Connecting you with me.

Walking the road to Ross by way of Inverness
By the One Above All, this land was truly blessed.
Rolling hills, royal thistles, and the great Scotch Pine.
My hearts in the Highlands,
But I'm just sitting here doing time

My heart's in the Highland,
    though my mind is somewhere else,
Among the cairns and bairns
    of the northernmost Celts,
North past the Roman wall,
    in the dwellings of the sìth,
My heart's in the Highlands,
Across the sea.

My heart's in the Highlands
    with Caledon and Cruithne's kin
You can't move forward
    without knowing where you've been
Oh, vagabond feet, wherever you roam
    Don't you know
These Highlands will always be your home?

*"I am yours, however distant you may be.
Your sorrow, when you grieve, brings grief to me.
There blows no wind but wafts your scent to me,
There sings no bird but calls your name to me.
Each memory that has left its trace with me
Lingers forever, as if part of me."*

>From *The Story of Layla and Majnun*
by Nizami Ganjavi
Translated by Rudolph Gelpke

I Am Yours

न त्वेवाहं जातु नासं न त्वं नेमे जनाधिपा
न चैव न भविष्याम: सर्वे वयमत: परम्

"*Never was there a time when I did not exist, nor you, nor all these kings; nor in the future shall any of us cease to be*"

Bhagavad Gita 2:12

To Whom It May Concern

There has never been a time
When I did not love you
And there never will be a time
When I cease to do so

We've been through so much together
We've faced it all:
Life and Death,
Death and Life
Love and Hate,
and Love again.

We've survived the pain and the tears
And enjoyed unquenchable laughter
Together there is nothing we cannot do

And though we are separated now
By more than miles
And less than death,
I am content, for I am yours,
No matter how distant,
No matter how far.

I am content.
For what was,
Will be once more.

Life is a circle, it has no end
Only infinite beginnings
And as long as there's life, there's hope
And as long as there's Love, I have you.

Ripples

You entered my life
Like a pebble tossed
Into a pond,
Sending ripples out
In all directions
In time & space.

All loves before you
Were shadowy premonitions.
All those after you
Incomplete echoes
That resonated and rhymed,
But could never replace.

All I loved
Were the parts of them
That reminded me of you

Freckles and Curls

In embryonic Eden
Before the rains came:
Seeds were planted,
Hand in hand,
Giving rise to fruit trees
Casting shadows
Over evermore.

In elementary Eden
Before the fruit was ripe:
A vision of paradise
With brown curls and freckles.
A déjà-vu unnoticed.

You pressed my back
against the chain link fence,
your lips touched mine;
I didn't know what I had,
but gladly I gave it
all to you.
You held it close to your heart,
And away you flew.

12-21-20

I found you
down on Salem Avenue
after the darkness fell.
Pavlov's pain prevented me
from telling you the truth:

That your smile,
and those freckles on your nose,
parted the clouds,
pulled back the curtain,
and loosened the tightness
in my chest.

Was that smile
just for me?
I'll probably never know.
Before I could ask
I was left alone again,
barefoot in the freshly
fallen snow.

There was that one time
at band camp
when the summer breeze
kissed the beach.
You made castles
in the sand.
We ate s'mores
By the bonfire,
brown curls
falling in your eyes,
freckles dancing
on your cheeks;
laughter that would never end.

In the fall
you wanted to make it official.
We set the time
and you saved the date,
but I forgot
and left you standing there
in front of the supermarket,
emerald eyes shedding
saltwater fears.

The last time
I saw you,
Outside that dancehall
Near Haystack Rock,
You couldn't even
Look me in the eye,
And I never looked back.

East of Eden
Before Death entered the world.
I saw you there,
Slouching in your desk
Across the classroom.

You came up behind me
As they walked on by,
Oblivious and annoyed.
We straggled behind,
Shoulder to shoulder,
Entangled forever.

A Different Kind of Treaty

My love doesn't ache anymore,
Though hearts still break,
Down the road
Amongst the souls
At the lost baggage counter.

We've had this conversation before,
And it never ends well.
A treaty
Written on scarred backs
With silent suffering.
Vocabulary chosen carefully
To soften the blows
And avoid civilian casualties.

My heart doesn't ache for you anymore,
Though my lips yearn for your touch.

Love is an old red barn
Stuffed with hay
And smelling of shit.
Housing many animals,
Mammals, and birds.
All looking quite different,
Yet all sprung from the same seed.

We've had this conversation before,
But it's never ended like this.
A treaty
Signed in blood
With no guarantees given.

Self-preservation,
Self-destruction;
A path out of the dark.

Finding our way,
Finding ourselves,
As the light leaves the park.

VIVĀMUS, MEA LESBIA, ATQVE AMEMVS,
RVMORESQUE SENVM SEVERIORVM
OMNES VNIVS AESTIMEMVS ASSIS!

*"Let us live and let us love, my Lesbia,
let us value to gossip of cranky old men
as one does a counterfeit ha'penny!"*

Gaius Valerius Catullus (c. 84-c. 54 BCE)
Translated from the Latin by John W Leys

Live and Love
(After Catullus V)

Let us live and let us love,
My Lesbia,
My Layla,
My dark princess of the nighttime sky,
Framed in velvet as black as raven's wings,
Illuminated by a thousand suns
Glowing through pinpricks
In the fabric of the night.

May we live and love
Free of the judgmental eyes
And gossip tongues
Which blow an ill wind,
Not worth a wooden nickel.

My Irish princess,
My Cornish queen,
Your king is in the counting house
Counting all his money,
While I'm deep in love
Counting all your kisses,
One for each light
In the heavenly vault.

Always

First thought; last thought
So many thoughts in between.
First love; last love
Nothing else seems real.

Always travels on two paths:
Future and Past,
Ripples on the water
Warping space-time in all directions,
In ten dimensions,
Entangled in infinity.

Last thought; first thought
A dream of two.
Last love; first love
It's always been you.

Tangled Up in You

Skin slick with sweat,
Pheromones fill the air.
Passions peak and dissipate.

Euphoria spreads,
Satiated; satisfied,
Sleeping wrapped
In each other's arms.

My Irish Princess

Porcelain Irish princess,
Goddess of the newborn sun,
Tresses of flame framing a face,
Dancing like dervishes in the wind.

Copper stars sprinkled
Across the milky white way,
Iridescent suns burning pink,
Glowing soft against alabaster clouds,
Flying low over the eastern sea.

"Now the darkness only stays the nighttime
In the morning it will fade away
Daylight is good at arriving at the right time
It's not always gonna be this grey
All things must pass
All things must pass away"
- George Harrison, 1970

All Things Must Pass

The Little Black Notebook

This little black notebook is almost full,
Each page covered in India Ink
scrawled verses and rhymes,
In an odd mixture of cursive and print
That would give a pharmacist pause,
Drops of blood in the margins
Mixing with the ink as it dries.

Memories and emotions,
Thoughts and despair.
Ideas and experiments,
Passions and Pain.
Captured forever by
A mystic binding spell
Of all nine muses.

Like all things
This notebook has an end.
There are only so many pages in its binding,
Only so many things to be written.
But for every end there is a beginning,
And a new notebook to open;

לאהוב אין סוף

Acknowledgments

First, once again, I would like to thank every person who bought, read, or reviewed a copy of *The Darkness of His Dreams* and *Whispers of a One-Eyed Raven*. Your support of my work means a lot. If you don't see your name below, please know that if you supported my writing in any way that I truly appreciate you.

Thank you to my son, Tristyn. You've always been very supportive of my writing, and I truly appreciate it. Thank you for every time over the last couple of years when you've asked "So, when's the next book coming out?" Also, thank you for the beautiful Granddaughter (Hello, Hadley!)

Thank you to my best friend, Misti, for your enthusiastic support for my creative endeavors and for your feedback on poems I text to you on occasion. I'm glad we found one another again.

If you like the photos and illustrations in this book, you should thank Misti, she encouraged it. If you don't like them, it's her fault!

Thank you to Elizabeth M Castillo, who was the first person to read 'Freckles and Curls' and gave me very helpful advice on it. She's a good friend and an amazing poet. *If you haven't bought her book yet, what's wrong with you?*

Thank you to Lindsey Heatherly for your friendship and support. *Lindsey also has a book out that you should get RIGHT NOW!*

Thank you to Cassie, Indy, and Leah. I hit a rough patch earlier this year and you three were instrumental in getting through it as smoothly as I did. I appreciate all of you.

Leah, you've truly made a difference in my life, I'm lucky to know you.

Thank you to Christine E Ray of Indie Blu(e) Publishing who invited me to help edit an anthology by and about poets and artists with mental illnesses (*Through the Looking Glass: Reflections on Madness and Chaos Within*) It was an honor to be asked and a pleasure to work with you and the Indie Blu(e) crew.

Thank you to my cousin Helen, who asked me to write something for her mom's funeral. It was an honor to be asked & it turned into one of the set pieces of this collection and helped inspire the title.

Thank you to Kindra M. Austin, a very talented poet, novelist, and editor. The feedback you give me is always well thought out and helpful.

Thank you to Kindra and Candice Louisa Daquin who both wrote pre-publication reviews for this book. They are both among my best friends and have helped me navigate the last few years of life changes. *They both have books that you should run out and buy immediately!!*

Thank you to Kristiana Reed for the Instagram writing prompt that inspired 'The Love Song of a Lost Raven.' *And yes, you should buy her books too!*

Are you making a list of books?
You should really make a list…

Thank you to the crew at Indie Blu(e) Publishing, who published 'Silence Falls,' Solitary Confinement,' 'Darkness and Fog,' and 'Defenses Down' in *Through the Looking Glass – Reflecting on the Madness and Chaos Within.*

Thank you to David L. O'Nan who first published 'It's Getting Darker' in his book *Avalanches of Poetry Inspired by Leonard Cohen.* It's an honor to be connected with Leonard's name in any way.

And finally, a very special thank you to Layla. If I could choose a place to die, it would be in your arms;

About The Author

John W. Leys was first moved to write song lyrics after being introduced to the Beatles and Bob Dylan when he was a teenager. A chance encounter with a radioactive fountain pen turned him into a ukulele playing poet, a curse he's had to live with for decades.

The greatest influences on his poetry have been Lord Byron, Leonard Cohen, Allen Ginsberg, Bob Dylan, Catullus, Erica Jong, and a chemical imbalance in his brain.

John's first poetry collection, *The Darkness of his Dreams,* was published in 2019. His second book, *Whispers of a One-Eyed Raven: Mythological Poetry,* followed the next year. He's also been published in anthologies from Indie Blu(e) Publishing, one of which he helped edit. He often wonders, in the third person, if anyone reads the *About the Author* section in books, or if he's just wasting his time trying to be clever.

When not writing poetry, John can usually be found playing one of his many ukuleles or feeding the crows & ravens in the park.

JohnWLeys.com   -   linktr.ee/johnwleys

Also from Broken Wing Publishing

Myths are stories without authors, composed before we wrote things down, when everything was recorded on the poet's tongue and in the bard's breath. They stem from a time when the border between dream and reality was barely drawn, when the wall between this world and the other was but a thin membrane, at best. Myths were our first attempts to make sense of the world around us, using inspiration and imagination, before the philosophers invented epistemology and the scientific method. They are stories that hold truths that linger in the darkened hallways and under the hollow hills, that enchant the imagination and stir the poet's heart. Whispers of a One-Eyed Raven is a collection of such stirrings. Join John W. Leys on a journey in verse through myths and legends to a time that never existed and will never end.

If you enjoyed the poems in The Lord of the Rings, *you're going to love* Whispers of a One-Eyed Raven. *Author John W. Leys writes in a style that feels inspired by classical poetry, blending mythological and fantasy elements to create something that feels not only authentic but also immensely enjoyable to read.*
    Pikasho Deka *for Readers' Favorite*

Leys has a way of drawing you into his world, keeping you engaged, and making you want to be in the world of old. He evokes emotion, imagery, and history. The languages were a great resource and anyone of Celtic ancestry or anyone interested in that culture would be wonderfully immersed in it. The poetry had a quite airy quality that keeps the reader involved, imagining, and wanting for more. I highly enjoyed Leys book and am sure to reference back to it when the mood strikes.
    Ruth Anne Garcia
    Poet/Author of *Bleeding Orchid: From Diagnosis to Remission: A Poetry Collection*

Also from Broken Wing Publishing

The Darkness of His Dreams is an intimate journey by way of verses—a sequence of poignant and thought-provoking ruminations. Readers will travel the ages through the keen lens that Leys has trained on history, philosophy, humanity, and his own life experiences. *The Darkness of His Dreams* is fine bourbon. Drink its words and feel pleasantly full.

"Leys is a poet whose work is imbued with lyrical rhythm. Throughout this book, Leys' words sing and his passion for the written word leaps from the page. Thus, Leys flits delicately between grief, melancholy, joy, cynicism, and hopeful hilarity. Leys is eclectic and he writes what he wants to write; a quality I admire greatly."

-Kristiana Reed, Author of *Flowers on the Wall*

"My favorite poem in The Darkness of His Dreams *is 'Kaddish for Karen Leys.' This piece is Leys bared soul at its best. The heart stunning loss of his beloved mother and the grief he feels is communicated with raw emotion and tenderness—my skin is chilled every time I read it."*

-Kindra M. Austin, Author of *I Am a War*

From Indie Blu(e) Publishing

Join 158 writers and artists from across the globe as they journey Through the Looking Glass to unveil the truth about life with mental illness. Diverse, raw, and urgent, the poetry, prose, and artwork in this anthology dig deep into the experience of living with depression, anxiety, bipolar disorder, and other neurodivergent conditions, as well as the challenges of loving someone who struggles with such an illness.

Full of hope and despair, acceptance and rebellion, the creativity contained within these pages reflects the reality that we cannot walk around or behind the looking glass, but must walk through it unflinchingly to educate, foster compassion, and reduce the stigma so often associated with mental illness.

"The poems collected in Through the Looking Glass *represent stories of human reality courageously told."*
        -Virginia Watts
          Author of *The Werewolves of Elk Creek*

www.ingramcontent.com/pod-product-compliance
Lightning Source LLC
Chambersburg PA
CBHW071247070526
44583CB00017B/2365